Truth

Tanya Lloyd Kyi

orca soundings

ORCA BOOK PUBLISHERS

National Library of Canada Cataloguing in Publication Data

Kyi, Tanya Lloyd, 1973-

Truth / Tanya Lloyd Kyi.

(Orca soundings)

ISBN 1-55143-265-X

I. Title. II. Series.

PS8571.Y52T78 2003   jC813'.6   C2003-910665-9

PZ7.K98Tr 2003

First published in the United States, 2003

Library of Congress Control Number: 2003105877

Summary: When a prominent local adult is killed at a teen house party, the whole school seems to know who is to blame, but no one will go to the police.

Orca Book Publishers gratefully acknowledges the support for its publishing programs provided by the following agencies: the Government of Canada through the Book Publishing Industry Development Program (BPIDP), the Canada Council for the Arts, and the British Columbia Arts Council.

Cover design: Christine Toller
Cover photography: Eyewire
Printed and bound in Canada

06 05 04 • 5 4 3 2

IN CANADA:
Orca Book Publishers
1030 North Park Street
Victoria, BC Canada
V8T 1C6

IN THE UNITED STATES:
Orca Book Publishers
PO Box 468
Custer, WA USA
98240-0468

To Min Trevor Kyi, with love.
TLK

Acknowledgements:

The author would like to acknowledge S.L. (aka "the boss") and Susan Adamson for their advice and encouragement.

Tanya Lloyd Kyi lives with her husband in Vancouver, B.C. *Truth* is her first novel. She would like to write another, but her hands are sore from playing ultimate (frisbee) and learning to wheelie drop on her mountain bike. She hopes to one day be responsible enough to own a dog.

Chapter One

The police are at my door at 3 a.m.

I watch from the top of the stairs as Dad goes stumbling through the house, tying his checkered robe. He flicks on the porch light and squints out the window. Then he jerks his head in surprise. He moves so quickly to open the door that he stubs his toe on the wooden hedgehog in the entranceway. He greets the police officer while standing on one foot like a giant plaid flamingo.

The officer doesn't smile. "Dr. Forester?" he asks. "I'm Officer Wells. I'd like to speak with your daughter for a moment."

"Jen?"

"There's been an accident at the Klassen house. I'm hoping she might answer some questions."

I'm wide awake. I'd climbed into bed when I got home, only to stare at the ceiling. I've spent the last two hours wondering if the doorbell would ring.

"What kind of accident?" Dad asks. "Jen was involved? Are you sure?"

When he's finally given time to answer, the officer sounds calm but firm. "Your daughter's not necessarily involved, sir. We're questioning everyone who was at the Klassen house this evening."

I don't want to hear him describe the accident. Without waiting for Dad to call me, I start down the stairs. For a minute I think I'm going to throw up. Instead, I take a deep breath and try to look sleepy and confused.

Dad motions us to the dining room table. Then he steps into the kitchen to make coffee. Despite the banging of spoons and cups, I can tell he's listening.

Officer Wells leans toward me. I feel like I've been sucked into the TV and I'm in an episode of *Law & Order*. I almost giggle. Then I almost throw up again. I tell myself to calm down. Breathe. This isn't nearly as easy as those TV criminals make it look. Those gold bars on his uniform and the baton in his belt and his coffee breath washing over me are all a bit intimidating.

"Miss Forester, we're dealing with a very serious case here. I'm sure I don't have to tell you how important it is for you to be completely honest."

"Of course." I'm thinking calm thoughts. Still breathing. And I have an excellent innocent look. I'm blonde, which I think helps. I open my eyes wide and look straight at Officer Wells. This strategy works wonders with my math teacher.

"You were at Ian Klassen's house party this evening?"

I nod.

"Could you tell me about it?"

"Georgia Findley and I went together. Another friend dropped us off. She had to be home before eleven, so she didn't stay. The party wasn't too exciting. We mostly sat around in the kitchen and talked all night. Jerome drove me home."

"What time did you leave?" he asks.

"About quarter to one. Curfew," I say, with an explanatory jerk of my head towards the kitchen. We can still hear my dad rummaging around.

"And Jerome is?"

"Jerome Baxter. My boyfriend."

He takes notes on all of this, then asks if I know Ted Granville.

"I don't think so. Why?"

"He's tall, red hair, about forty. Did you see anyone like that at the party tonight?"

"No. What happened?"

"He was badly beaten — may not survive."

I expected that, but I put on my most shocked expression. It's not entirely fake. "It was all kids there, I think. I was in the kitchen for most of the night, not by the door. I didn't see anyone like that come in."

It's true, what I tell official Officer Wells, leaning towards me like we're buddies from way back. Technically, it's all true.

But there's more to it. I had run upstairs with everyone else after Candi Bherner had run down screaming. We weren't expecting much. Candi's younger than me, and I don't know her well, but she seems totally flaky. A mouse could have made her scream like that.

It wasn't a mouse. It was a redheaded man sprawled across the floor in Ian's parents' room, one arm up as if he'd rolled out of bed. His arm was twisted, and the back of his head was wet with blood.

Just breathe, I tell myself as I drum my fingernails on the dining room table. Don't think about it. If you think about it, Officer Wells is going to know. And he doesn't know anything. He's not looking for you anyway. I make my fingers stop tapping.

It's true that Officer Wells doesn't know anything. He seems at a bit of a loss, slumping slightly now, his eyes wandering around the dining room and across to the living room.

Both rooms are spectacularly ugly. So ugly that I once entered a home makeover contest that I found in one of Georgia's mom's magazines. No luck, though. The house is still hideous. I can imagine my mom and dad decorating it together when they moved here. I can see them choosing the rust-colored shag and the wood paneling and the couch with its wagon wheel upholstery. They must have thought they were at the height of fashion. That was the seventies. I was born in the eighties; my mom left in the nineties. The wood paneling and the wagon wheels live on.

It's all too much for Officer Wells. Just as my dad finally has the coffee ready, the officer stands, shakes hands with both of us, and prepares to leave.

"I'll be in touch if I need to speak with you again."

Ian's party was the most exciting news to sweep the school since the computer science teacher was charged with assault. He pushed his ex-wife into a table at one of our town's two bars. That was months ago.

The booming metropolis of Fairfield (population: 5,000; things to do: 0) is in a mountain valley. We're over an hour from the nearest mall and two hours from the closest town with a movie theater. About a zillion hours from anything else of interest. Sticksville, British Columbia. My dad grew up in Vancouver. He says he and Mom moved here because they wanted to raise their children (who turned out to be just me) in a more peaceful place. Well, it's definitely peaceful. So peaceful the whole population could knock off in their sleep and the outside world would never know.

In the summer we entertain ourselves with bush parties. That's when a few guys throw some wood in the back of a pickup, drive out to the old gravel pits or the banks of the river and light a bonfire. Then people spread the word — usually in the 7-Eleven parking lot. We stash a bottle of vodka down the side panel of Georgia's ancient Honda (the plastic door-handle part pulls right off) and drive out in search of the party.

That's the summer. In the winter we rent movies (yawn), hang out at Willie's Chicken until it closes at eleven (double yawn), and basically try to fight off death by boredom. So when Ian mentioned that his parents were spending the first two weeks of November in Mexico, we were buzzing around him like a swarm of starving bees. Ross Reed spent a whole week telling people about the party before Ian said it was okay. Poor Ian is one of those really nice people who's easily pushed around. There wasn't much he could do.

Ross organizes most of Fairfield's parties. He knows everyone. Wherever he goes, the party goes. I think his life revolves around weight lifting and beer. Maybe it's hereditary — everyone says Ross's mom OD'd on pills after his dad took off. Now Ross lives with his grandmother.

Rumor has it Ross and some of his friends are on 'roids. It's probably true because they spend tons of time at the gym. Nate's on the junior hockey team and says he wants to make it to the NHL. Ross doesn't play any sports — I think he just likes being big. He walks like a bodybuilder, with his arms held out from his body as if he'd like to put them down, but his muscles get in the way.

Last summer Ross picked a fight at a bush party with somebody's cousin visiting from the Okanagan. When the guy had been harassed enough, he swung hard, sending Ross's head whipping back. Ross recovered and lunged at him. Suddenly the Okanagan guy was off balance, wheeling towards the fire. Somebody pulled him out of the flames and someone else drove him to the hospital after. I heard that his parents called the cops, and they interviewed Ross, but nothing happened. That's Ross — he gets away with everything.

The afternoon after the fire incident, a bunch of us were hanging out at Georgia's, too sluggish to want to do anything. Jerome was there (we'd just started seeing each other then), and Nate and Ross. Georgia gave Ross a wet tea bag and told him to put it on his eye, black and swollen from the fight. Ross took a black scarf off the back of Georgia's bedroom door and tied it around his head to hold the tea bag. When Georgia's mom came home from her golf game, rather than take the scarf off and reveal his black eye, Ross spent the rest of the afternoon talking like a pirate, answering all questions with "Aye, matey." He called Jerome his parrot. So despite the poor guy from the Okanagan, who we heard had third-degree burns on his leg, it was, as always, really hard not to forgive Ross.

That's what churns through my head as I sit at the table after Officer Wells has been shown out the door. My dad sits down across from me.

"So?" he asks.

It's hard for me to lie to my dad. He raises his bushy eyebrows and looks at me like I know he must look at the patients at his doctor's office — with some wise-seeming mixture of sympathy and authority.

"Some old guy got really beat up tonight. I didn't know him and I didn't see who beat him up. Georgia and I heard about it and we left."

"Ted Granville runs the credit union," he tells me, proving that he was listening to the whole conversation.

"Weird," I say. "I don't know what he was doing at the party."

My dad nods slowly. "Stay home tomorrow. I don't want you running around town," he says. "And get some sleep."

Like I can sleep.

Chapter Two

Ted Granville died. When I get to school on Monday morning, the first group of kids I see is talking about the murder. And the second group. And the third. By the time I reach my locker, I've heard: (a) everyone at the party was on acid, freaked out, and killed Ted Granville; (b) Ted Granville came over with a gun to break up the party, and three guys beat him up in self-defense; and (c) Ted

Granville went crazy, leapt off the second- floor balcony and broke his neck on the pavement of the driveway. As far as I can remember, Ian's house doesn't even have a balcony.

My only reliable source is Georgia, whose mom knows Mrs. Granville. She's been at the Granvilles' house all weekend, helping look after the two little kids.

"What have you heard?" Georgia asks as soon as she sees me.

"I've heard a zillion rumors already," I tell her, "but no one seems to know what really happened."

As usual, Georgia looks like a movie star who got trapped in high school by mistake. Red hair perfectly in place, pierced belly button peeking out over low-cut jeans, and just a faint red rim around her eyes. She's obviously been crying, but when I cry my face looks like it's been run over by a tractor. Life is totally unfair.

She sniffs delicately. "My mom says he died in the ambulance on the way to the hospital. Massive head injuries."

"Did you see the blood on the floor?"

She nods, making a face. "I can still picture it if I close my eyes."

"What was he doing at the party?"

"Mom said he was a family friend. Ian's parents had asked him to keep an eye on the house."

Then the bell rings and there's no time for more details.

In homeroom we hear that our principal Mr. Seorgel — a.k.a. Snoregel — has called a school assembly. No big surprise. I'm just glad I'm not the one who has to cover assemblies for the school news show. They're usually one big snoozefest.

A few years ago, one of the teachers got permission to run a student-operated news and sports hour on the Fairfield cable station. It airs once a week and the entire student population seems to tune in — maybe for the gossip factor.

I worked on the show all last year. This year I'm a lead reporter. My big stories so far are:

"Is Shoplifting on the Rise?"

"Joe Jobs — the Good, the Bad, and the Cash."

"Exposé! A Day in the Life of a Fairfield Basketball Star."

The research for that last one was pretty fun. But Ms. Chan, the sponsor teacher, says I need to start working on more serious stories. "Dig for the truth," she said a few weeks ago. At the time I thought the concept of real news happening in Fairfield was pretty funny.

Making my way through the hordes to the assembly, I see Jerome coming towards me. He's tall — just over six feet — and his hair is pale, pale blond. He's easy to spot. Not hard to look at, either. When he first asked me out last spring, I was so excited there was a perma-grin stuck to my face for a week.

"Did the cops come to your house?"

"At three in the morning," I tell him. "I was dying to call you yesterday, but Dad decided it was father-daughter quality time. All long, long, boring day! Did they talk to you?"

"Yeah. Mom freaked. What did you tell them?"

"Basically nothing. You?"

"Same. They weren't the sharpest knives in the drawer anyway. The cops here are either mean or stupid."

"Think so?"

"Remember last year, when Ross was driving drunk and they tried to pull him over? He outran them for long enough to make a run for it. Then he called his grandmother from a pay phone and told her some kid had just stolen the car. She believed him *and* the cops believed him. Or at least they couldn't prove otherwise."

By this time we're in the gym and Snoregel is at the mike. When he gets everyone quiet, it goes something like "unmatched tragedy . . . condolences to friends and familypolice investigation . . . full cooperation . . . "

Jerome leans over partway through the speech. "Listen, Ross is worried the cops are going to hassle him because of that fight last summer. You'll stay cool about it, right?"

"Of course." When I think about it, Ross

was at the party when I came in, but I don't remember seeing him after I saw the body. I was probably in shock. I try to remember who was with me in the bedroom. Candi had screamed her way downstairs. Georgia ran up with me. Ian was there, looking like a ghost. I guess having to explain a dead guy to your parents is a little worse than them finding out about your house party.

Who else? Jerome. I know there were more, but everyone else is a bit of a blur. It was Nate who took control of the situation. He walked in and within seconds the world was moving again. He sent Ian to phone 911 and told everyone else to clear out. That's what we did. Fast.

"Listen, tell Georgia to stay cool too, okay?"

I nod absently. Officer Wells is at the microphone now. He's way taller than Snoregel and has trouble adjusting the microphone. He tries to stoop towards it and look up at the bleachers at the same time.

He tells us how important any information will be in the next few days. How all tips will remain confidential, etc. It sounds suspiciously like my dad's customary weekend speech: "If you ever need a ride home, just call. There will be no questions asked." Who believes that speech? Not even my dad, who's pretty laid-back in general, can pull off that one.

Georgia catches up to me in the hallway after the assembly. "Listen," she says, "I was talking to Nate and he asked if we could keep as cool as possible about this whole thing. You know, don't talk about it too much at school and stuff."

I shrug. "Sure. Jerome said the same thing."

The rest of the morning is a write-off. I drift through my classes until lunch. Then I remember I have a news team meeting.

On a scale of 1 to 10, where 10 is supremely cool and 1.5 is about as cool as the average teacher gets, Ms. Chan is at least an 8. She's the sponsor teacher of our TV show

— *Fair Game*. The show runs on Fairfield's local cable channel every Friday after school. It's supposed to be like a news program, with an anchor introducing different reporters "on location." Usually there's one feature and a couple of short clips.

Before she became a teacher, Ms. Chan was a reporter in Ontario. I can totally picture her with a tape recorder in one hand and a microphone in the other, following a lawyer down the stairs of the courthouse to get a comment. She looks like she should be on TV too. She has bobbed black hair, nice clothes, heels that click, click across the lab.

The media lab is actually an office at the back of Ms. Chan's classroom. There are a few chairs, a couple of big tables and two computer desks where we do our video editing.

At our Monday meeting we divvy up assignments. This week there are the usual sports updates, a profile of the new art teacher and an exposé on whether men's and women's razors are actually different. The main story is a special feature on the murder investigation. That one's mine.

I sit for a minute after the meeting breaks up, organizing my thoughts. What would I most want to know if I was listening to the news? I'd want to know if Officer Wells was going to turn up at my house again. Maybe more about how they do a murder investigation. And the main thing: who was the murderer?

That stops me. It's like I've been refusing to think about it since Saturday night. Now there's the giant question mark jumping at me from my notebook. Who killed Ted Granville? I was there, I should be able to figure it out. More than that — I should already know!

Some people are always the last to know everything, but I'm the first. Too much time on the phone and an overdeveloped sense of gossip, I guess. I love secrets. When Georgia's mom was pregnant last year (can you imagine getting pregnant when you're forty-five?), I was the only one other than Georgia who knew for three whole months. When that girl in grade ten moved away, who was the first to find out that her neighbors thought her dad was in the KKK? Me. Even though it turned out to be a lie. That's all part of being a good journalist. I have to sniff out rumors and check the facts.

So why don't I know this?

By the time I've finished wondering, everyone's gone except Scott Rich, our best camera operator. Ms. Chan has assigned him to get some crime scene shots.

Scott's unusual in our school — he's actually interesting. He's only in grade eleven, but he seems like the sort of old philosopher that you'd find living in a mountain cave. He's got shoulder-length, curly hair that he mostly wears in a ponytail, and it seems like he always has a video camera with him. He says he's an observer of humanity. I swear he's achieved a Zen state at age sixteen.

The other day we were all hanging out at lunchtime in the courtyard of the school, and Georgia and Nate were arguing about what "mellow" music was.

"Melancholy," was Georgia's answer.

"You mean sappy, my-boyfriend-dumped-me songs," Nate said. "That's not it at all. It's tempo."

Then they saw Scott walking by the door and they pulled him outside and into the debate.

He tilted his head to the side for a second. "Passive," he said and left. And everyone else sat there nodding.

Anyway, it's always interesting to work on a story with Scott. On one hand, he makes me a bit nervous. I might not live up to his transcendental vision of the world. On the other, he sees things that I would otherwise miss.

We arrange to walk over to Ian's house — the "scene of the crime" — after school together. Scott can get some shots, and I can grill any investigators that are hanging around.

Lucky for me, the first police officer I see is Dave McBride. He plays tennis with my dad in the summers. He's just on his way to his car when we see him. I'm happy to find him outside because I really, really don't want to ring the doorbell and talk to Mr. and Mrs. Klassen. They can't possibly be in a good mood right now.

"Officer McBride!" I call, and Scott follows behind as I run up to the police car. "Can you give me any info on the investigation? I'm covering the story for the school news."

"Hey, Jen!" he greets me with a big smile. "Don't know how much I can tell you. You should call the detachment and they'll put you through to our press contact."

"And what will he tell me?"

"Oh, general stuff. The victim is Ted Granville, local banker, 43 years old, father of two elementary school kids. The force is dedicating its full attention to the investigation."

"And what does that mean?" I ask. "How exactly do you investigate? I thought there would be police all over the place, but you're the only one here."

"The more officers you have, the more likely someone will disturb the scene. I stopped by to make sure everything was secure, but there's an investigator inside finishing up the real work."

"And what's that?"

"He photographs everything, makes notes of blood splatters and body position, looks for signs of the struggle, collects the major evidence."

"Does any of it point to a killer?" I hold my breath.

"Sorry. Can't release that information to the press."

"Off the record?" I say hopefully. I glance back at Scott. He takes the hint and wanders away, turning the camera toward the house.

"I really shouldn't be discussing it…" he says, but I detect a hint of wavering.

I think fast. "Of course I'd never tell anyone. But I watch all those cop shows on TV, and the way they collect their evidence is *so* amazing." Am I overdoing it? I hold my breath.

"It's an art form," Officer McBride agrees.

"Fascinating. Can you give me an example?" My eyelashes have never been batted so quickly in their entire eyelash lives.

"Hypothetically?" Officer McBride says.

"Of course."

"Well, we might see a partial boot print in the blood at the scene. We can compare that to prints on file — find out that it's not a regular shoe."

"Really? Is that what happened here? You have a distinctive print?" I try to keep my excitement out of my voice.

Officer McBride looks uncomfortable. "I was speaking theoretically," he says. "And not a word of that to anyone."

"Scout's honor," I tell him (which doesn't count for much, since I quit after three weeks of Brownies).

I grab Scott and prepare to scram, but just then a second officer comes out of the house and strides towards us.

"You kids looking for something?" he asks. He's tall and thick like a stereotypical cop. Beside him, Scott looks like a stringbean.

"Just getting some footage for the school news show."

He leans towards us. "I hope you're not involved in any of this."

We shake our heads in unison.

"I'd better not find out otherwise."

We smile as if he's joking, but he doesn't smile back. He turns and struts off towards Officer McBride's car.

"Power trip" is Scott's assessment as we leave.

When I get home, I've had enough of cops for the day. Still, I call the detachment and the receptionist faxes a press update to the machine in my dad's den. I start to skim through, and it says almost exactly what Officer McBride said it would. Then something catches my eye.

"At present, the detachment is investigating the possibility that more than one assailant may have been involved in the attack."

Chapter Three

Here's a diary of my hellish Thursday:
8:15 a.m.
Georgia's on-again, off-again crush on Nate is definitely on at the moment. Personally, I don't see what's so attractive about a hockey jersey, but the girl's obsessed. I'm trying to talk to her about the murder before the homeroom bell rings, but she's not paying attention. She's scanning the hallway, hoping to spot Nate.

"We had lunch in the courtyard together twice last week, but this week he's totally avoiding me," she complains.

"I don't know what you see in him," I tell her. "Jerome says he's on steroids. Probably can't even get it up. Steroids do that, you know."

"Oh, and you have so much experience in that area."

She's got me there. I think Jerome's been expecting things to heat up soon, and I haven't decided yet what to do about that.

"Whether he can get it up or not, you still shouldn't be following him around like a puppy dog. He's not worth it."

"I'm not following him around."

I give her my "you're not fooling any-one" look.

"Listen, Nate's one of those guys who doesn't say much. But when he does, the whole room tunes in because it's important."

That's true. Especially when I think about how Nate took control at the party. Before I can tell Georgia that, he's walked by and she's left me in the dust to skip along beside him. Waiting for his next words of wisdom, I guess.

8:25 a.m.

It's a relief to be alone for a few minutes. I've been up late the last two nights writing my news script. It turned out to be a basic summary of facts — the usual who, what, when and where. Except the "who" is only who was murdered, not who did the murdering.

I slide down to sit on the floor, leaning back to rest against my locker. With each sentence I've written, this whole situation has become more real. A man died. Was killed. Is dead. The stomach ache I had the night of the party has come back on a permanent basis.

As the murder gets more real, school gets more surreal. Everyone's back to chatting and laughing and, in Georgia's case, boy chasing, like nothing ever happened.

I close my eyes for a minute. When I open them, it's because I can feel someone standing over me.

"Hey, Jen."

It's Ross, his hair still damp from the shower. He squats in front of me, his knees on either side of mine, his hand pressed against the locker above my shoulder for balance. I'm caged by his body, and he's close enough that I can smell his deodorant.

"What happened at Ian's blows, huh?"

I nod, though this is the understatement of the century. The bell rings, and people start to sort themselves into their homerooms.

"Poor Ian's grounded for life. Might be allowed out when he's forty."

This time I give him an obligatory smile, but I'm feeling weird. Ross and I are friendly, but we don't talk a lot. He's Jerome's friend more than mine. And he's suffocating me. "I should get to class."

"Lots of time. Relax," he says and leans even closer. "Jerome tells me you're doing a news report about the situation."

"For the school show, yeah."

"Anything I should know about?"

"That depends. Are you the news police?

A journalist never gives up her sources, you know." I'm joking. Ross is starting to bug me, but I'm one hundred percent joking. The look he gives me is completely serious.

"Let's just say I'm an interested member of your audience."

"It's just the official facts from the police. Were you even there? I don't remember seeing you afterwards."

He shakes his head. "Booked out early. Heard there was another party."

"So what's the big deal then?"

"Just don't want trouble. I gotta go."

He unfolds himself and lopes off down the hall, long legs disappearing around the corner. So much for social graces. The final bell rings and I'm still sitting in the hallway. Sighing, I pull myself up and head to the office for a late slip.

Noon

The day is getting progressively worse. I have no friends at lunch. Georgia goes off with Nate. Jerome says he has to talk to Ross about something and disappears. I don't even get a chance to tell him how weird Ross was this morning. With nothing else to do, I head to the media lab, where Ms. Chan asks if we can talk about my piece.

"It's good, Jen. All the facts are there. But I think you're missing some of the human element. What did Ted Granville's neighbors think of him? Is he well-known in Fairfield? What about comments from the partygoers?

"I'm not saying this story isn't worth running," she continues. "It is. But let's follow it up next week with both a factual update and some people's reactions. Sound okay?"

I nod, mostly to get her to go away. She's great, but this day has Murphy's Law written all over it.

2:30 p.m.

I forgot to do my reading last night, so I flunk the pop quiz Mr. Johnson gives us on *Macbeth*. In retaliation, he makes me read part of Act V.

Mr. Johnson reads the part of a doctor, who has come to watch Lady Macbeth sleepwalk. I'm supposed to read Lady Macbeth's lines. It seems that after plotting and scheming with her husband, she's finally feeling a bit of post-murder guilt. Stumbling around in her sleep, she sees blood on her hands. Out, out, damned spot, etc. After the first couple of minutes, I start to get into it. I'm rubbing my hands together in front of me, pretending they smell bad.

And here's where my day gets really putrid. All of a sudden I'm convinced that the whole class thinks I killed Ted Granville. Which is ridiculous. Completely unfounded. Half of them don't even know I was at the party. I tell myself to calm down, but someone coughs in the back, then I see two girls in the front look at each other. I'm convinced they're all thinking the same thing. Guilty. Guilty. I can't get the thought out of my head and I trash the rest of my lines. Then I say I have to go to the bathroom, grab my books and run out of the class.

I am such a freak.

3:30 p.m.

The final announcements, over the P.A.:

"There are messages in the office for blah blah, blah blah, blah blah, Jen Forester, blah blah..."

My message is from the school counselor. It says I should come to her office if I ever want to talk.

4:00 p.m.

At least the counselor gave me a choice. The police — Officer Wells and the investigator I saw at the crime scene — knock on the door almost as soon as I get home. They want me to come to the station to talk to them. I don't seem to have any say in the matter.

I feel like a criminal in the back of the police car, with its glass shield in front of me and its doors that don't open from the inside. At least I'm not handcuffed. When we get to the station, they leave me in a grungy room. My dad's on his way to meet us apparently.

After a long wait, all three of them file in. My dad gives me a worried look, but he squeezes my hand as he sits beside me. Officer Wells sits across from us. The other officer — Behnson turns out to be his name

— paces around the room. He's the one who asks questions. After a while it starts to make me dizzy to watch him as I answer.

I tell them the same things I told Officer Wells when he came to my house. I was in the kitchen all night. I never saw Ted Granville come in. Jerome drove me home.

When we've gone through it once, Behnson starts asking the same questions in different order. "Just to clarify," he says. Really I think he's trying to confuse me. He even gets some of the things wrong, which I'm sure is on purpose.

"So you were in the living room for most of the night?" he asks.

"The kitchen."

"And the body was upstairs?"

"I guess so."

"You never saw it?"

"No."

"Miss Forester, would it surprise you that other witnesses say that you were in the room with them when they discovered the body?"

It does surprise me. Although it

shouldn't. Of course they're interviewing everyone else who was there. We should have worked out a story so we all gave the same information. I can't think with everyone staring so hard at me. I rest my forehead on the table for a minute.

"Jen, did you lie to the police that night?" That's my dad questioning me now.

I lift my head up and shrug. "I didn't know he was dead. I just gave the simplest story I could. I expected this to all blow over."

"So you lied," Behnson says.

I nod.

"What made you go upstairs?"

"Candi ran down screaming. A bunch of us rushed up to see what was going on."

"Who was there?"

"Me, Georgia, Jerome, Nate… other people too, but I don't remember."

"Where was Ross Reed at this point?"

"I saw him earlier that night, but I don't think he was still there."

"Ian Klassen?"

"He was there."

"And where was the body when you found it?"

"On the floor in Ian's parents' bedroom. Kind of to the left of the bed."

"Who called the police?"

"Ian did. Nate told him to."

My dad starts to get impatient. "Look, Jen got scared and she lied. But she clearly wasn't involved in the attack."

"Just a few more questions, Dr. Forester. Jen, what did Candi tell you she'd seen upstairs?"

"She didn't tell me anything. She just screamed, and we ran up."

It goes on like this for another half an hour. Finally, when I feel my head is going to explode, they stop.

"We'll be in touch if we need any more information."

My dad leaves the room ahead of me, talking to Officer Wells about something. Officer Behnson grabs my arm as I head for the door. "You could be in a lot of trouble, young lady. If I find out you've lied again, we're going to go a lot further towards seeing *exactly* how you were involved in this."

I stumble out in a daze. My dad looks half worried and half angry, but I'm too tired to ask whether he's mad at me or at the cops. We drive home in silence.

Chapter Four

I get my usual morning kiss from Jerome at my locker, but he only stays a second.

"Gotta run," he says. "Didn't finish my math, and Nate promised to let me copy the last few questions before homeroom."

"Sure," I say, even though we've barely seen each other all week. "Are we still on for tonight?"

Jerome and I have a standing Friday

night date. Sometimes we go to a party or spend time with Ross and Nate and whatever bimbos they happen to be into that week. (The bimbo designation doesn't apply to Georgia, obviously.) Sometimes we just hang around one of our living rooms and watch movies.

"Oh, I meant to tell you, I can't make it." Jerome's already backing down the hall.

"What?"

"I have to run. Sorry. Listen, I'll call you on the weekend."

"Dick." I swear at him under my breath. Then I turn around to open my locker and bump into Georgia, who's standing behind me.

"Dick," she agrees. "Nate, too."

"What's happened now?"

"Same old thing. Yesterday he meets me for lunch, today he says he's busy all weekend and he'll catch me next week."

We give boys-are-stupid shakes of our heads.

"Georgia, you know how, when you do

something totally humiliating, it helps to tell everyone you know?" I ask her. "You give them the gory details, they agree that you're a nutbar, but they still love you?"

She nods.

"Well, I told you about my Lady Macbeth freak-out on Wednesday, but who else am I supposed to tell? Jerome's turned into a freak himself. Anyone else would probably send me off to the mental ward. My dad would have me to a shrink so fast you'd have to put up missing person posters."

"There's only one solution," she says.

"Drop English and don't graduate?"

"Nope. Fashion police. We've got ten minutes before the bell rings."

This is a mean game. But it's the best mood-improver since shopping, and there's no mall in Fairfield.

It started when Georgia and I met the first day of grade ten. She was obviously a new kid. First, because I've gone to school here since kindergarten and I didn't recognize her. And it's not just that I recognize everyone else in school. I know everything about them. I know that Ian Klassen peed on the teeter-totter at lunchtime in grade one. I know Nate is the youngest of three kids and the other two are practically geniuses. I know who's related and I know the complete dating history of every student. That's what happens when you go to school with the same people for thirteen years — you absorb their entire lives by osmosis. A few of us even went to preschool together.

So I knew Georgia had just moved here. The other thing that made me notice her was an amazing pair of high, black, leather boots. Something you can't buy within a five-hour shopping radius of Fairfield.

She was leaning against the locker beside mine when I walked up. (It turned out her last name was Findley, so we were alphabetically destined to be beside each other.)

"Great boots," I said.

"Thanks," she said, "but I was thinking of trading them in for a pair of those." She nodded towards a guy down the hall.

I turned around, and there was some poor

little grade eight kid who must have been sent to school in his sister's hand-me-down running shoes. They were covered in mud — probably a disguise strategy — but they were still an unmistakable pastel pink.

"Ouch," I said.

"Call the fashion police. Code red emergency."

And that's how the game started. As I said, it's not exactly a nice game. I'm sure it wasn't the poor kid's fault he had to wear pink shoes to school.

Today, Georgia looks like she stepped out of *Cosmo*. She grew up in the city and didn't want to move when her dad got a job here a couple of years ago. That, combined with the new baby last year (which still weirds us out), has somehow guilted her mom into giving Georgia her credit card number for internet shopping. Some people are blessed at birth. I complained to my dad once about not having enough clothes, and he suggested I take a sewing course. Ach!

"Code red! Code red!" Georgia whispers

from the corner of her mouth. We're both leaning back against the lockers, trying to act casual. "Look at that girl's shirt."

"It looks like it used to be her bedroom curtains," I giggle. "Hey, code blue on the acid wash jean jacket. Circa 1980."

Within five minutes I'm feeling way better.

"Speaking of code reds," Georgia says, "have you seen the shoes Ross has been wearing?"

"No, why?"

"He used to have these wicked Australian leather boots that his aunt sent him. Remember?"

"Yeah. He wears them every day."

"Not anymore. He's wearing disgusting runners. I asked what happened to the boots and he said they ripped."

I nod, but then something clicks in my head.

"Hey, Georgia," I say as the bell rings and we file towards homeroom, "when did they rip?"

"Don't know," she shrugs. "Not long ago."

"Does leather rip?" I wonder out loud, but the morning announcements start, and Georgia doesn't hear me.

I try to corner Jerome at his locker before lunch. He grimaces when he sees me.

"What, no kiss?" I ask.

"Sorry, Jen. I've gotta go."

"We need to talk."

"Sure. We'll set up some time on the weekend."

"We need to talk today."

"Okay. I'll be home after school. Call me then, okay?"

I nod, and he ducks out like someone who narrowly escaped prison.

Dad's not usually home from work until after five. I let myself in the house and rummage in the fridge for some leftover pasta. Then I wait half an hour to give Jerome time to get home. As I wait, I get more and more angry. Prick.

Who is he to brush me off like some clingy bimbo? It's not like I usually follow him around the hallways. Not like I practice Georgia's sick-puppy-following-Nate act. He's my boyfriend. When I need to talk to him, he's supposed to talk. Not pencil me in.

I call at exactly four o'clock. By that time, I'm so mad I have to clench my teeth to talk. Stay calm, I tell myself. Calm and cold. Ice queen.

"Hello. Is Jerome there, please?"

"Jen, it's me."

"Oh, I'm sorry. I must not recognize your voice anymore."

"Don't be ridiculous."

"I hardly think I'm being ridiculous. You refuse to talk to me at school. I haven't seen you all week. And then you break our date for tonight."

Silence.

"If you want to break up, you just have to say so."

"I don't want to break up," he says.

"Well, I might," I say, clenching my teeth

even harder so I won't cry. I'm definitely not going to cry.

"Jen, I'm sorry. This really has nothing to do with you. It's just that Ross is in some hot water and he doesn't want us talking to a lot of people."

"I'm a lot of people?"

More silence.

"You think I have a big mouth. That I'm going to tell everyone everything."

"No, I don't think that."

"You shouldn't. Because I haven't told people things. And there are things I could tell. I know about the boots, Jerome."

"What?"

"I know that two people were involved in the beating. I know that one of them had boots with unusual tread patterns. I know that Ross got rid of his boots after the party."

"Who else knows?"

"No one. But they'll figure it out soon, especially with you guys walking around like the secret service."

"Let me ask you something," he says.

"Say you and your dad are driving downtown late at night and you start arguing with him. It's dark, it's raining and he's distracted. He runs a red light. Wham! You hit another car, some Joe Blow driving home from the late shift. Killed instantly. When the police come, do you tell them what really happened, or do you tell them Joe Blow's the one that ran the red light?"

"I've heard this one before. And I'd tell them what really happened," I say.

"Joe's already dead. You're not going to change that by sending your dad to prison. It was an accident. Plus, you're partly at fault."

"How?"

"You started the argument. You distracted him."

"My dad wouldn't want me to lie about what happened."

"What if he did? What if he asked you to?"

"He wouldn't."

There's silence for a while. Finally Jerome says he should go.

"One more thing," I say.

"Yeah?"

"Ted Granville was beaten by two people. If Ross was one of them, that leaves Nate . . . or you."

He doesn't say anything for a long minute. Then: "Look, I've already had a really shitty day."

"Jerome, I think you can consider us broken up." With that, I hang up the phone.

My dad comes home a while later to find me bawling. You'd think they would train doctors to deal with crying people, but apparently not.

"Are you hurt?" he asks.

"No." Sniff.

"Okay," he says, and he pats me awkwardly on the shoulder a couple of times.

"Jerome and I broke up," I tell him.

"I'm sorry to hear that," he says, but I can tell he's not. Not entirely sorry, anyway. I stomp upstairs and slam my bedroom door. I only feel slightly better, so I open it and slam it again. Then I go to bed and don't get up until noon on Saturday.

Chapter Five

Anchor: Good afternoon, and welcome to this week's edition of *Fair Game*. Our lead story this week is the continuing police investigation into the murder of local banker Ted Granville.

Switch location to street in front of Ian's house.

Me: Fairfield police continue to interview students and community members, searching for leads in the murder of local banker Ted Granville. I'm here with Officer Tran.

Tran: Granville died of head injuries at the home of Jane and George Klassen on the evening of Friday, November 15. The Klassens were out of town at the time of the murder. The home was in the care of their son Ian, a grade twelve student at Fairfield Secondary.

Me: Will police continue to dedicate their full attention to the case?

Tran: We are giving this incident the highest priority and are dedicating all necessary resources to the investigation.

Me: What message would you offer to the students of Fairfield Secondary?

Tran: More than one person was involved in this crime and we believe others may have witnessed it. Students with any information should report it immediately to the police. The department has also established an anonymous tip line and posted details throughout the school.

Me: Police are unable to name suspects

at this time, but say they are investigating the movements of several persons of interest.

Anchor: The community continues to react with shock and outrage. Here's what Fairfield Secondary students and teachers had to say about the incident:

Switch to various hallway location shots.

Katy Gill: It's totally shocking. I always thought stuff like this just happened on TV or in big cities, not in towns like this.

Brent White: This could almost erase Fairfield's reputation as most boring town on earth.

Mr. Finn, Vice-Principal: I can only hope that our students will consider the severity of this event and offer their full cooperation to the authorities.

Jessie Scribes: Bad deal for that Granville dude, man.

I finished my police interview on the weekend and collected the student comments after the planning meeting on Monday. The piece is going to run with some of Scott's best video of the Klassen house. He took it from really low, so the house is silhouetted against some dark clouds. It looks really spooky — definitely like a murder site.

Ms. Chan is pleased with my piece. She should be. I spent a long time on it. I had nothing else to do all weekend except mope. Georgia was saintly enough to come over and keep me company on Saturday night. She arrived with more news — Jerome, Nate, Ross and Ian have all been questioned three times by the police. The latest interrogations were on Friday afternoon.

"I guess that's what Jerome meant when he said he'd had a really shitty day," I told her.

Georgia had rented three girl movies, and we sniffed our way through two of them. In between scenes she tried to comfort me.

"Whatever he's done, I'm sure he'll regret it tomorrow. He'll probably call and apologize, and everything will be back to normal."

"I don't think so." I shook my head. "It's a bit more complicated than that."

Georgia didn't say anything, and I could tell she was waiting for me to explain. I knew I should tell her about how Jerome had been avoiding me, about his "what if?" car accident questions, about the boot print and the evidence of two attackers. I opened my mouth to explain, but it all suddenly seemed too complicated. And the gist of it was that my boyfriend — ex-boyfriend — could be a murderer. That sounded so ridiculous that I couldn't say it.

Georgia waited expectantly while all these thoughts shot through my head like a laser light show. I was too tired to make any sense of them.

"I can't explain it all right now."

Her shoulders stiffened, and she looked away.

"I'm sorry," I started, but she interrupted me.

"No. No need to talk until you're ready. I'm sorry I pried."

I could tell she was hurt. She gathered up her stuff and left soon after.

I'm dreading bumping into Jerome in school, but I only see him once all day. He's leaning against his locker and joking with a group of guys. He looks like everything's normal, which makes me want to punch him. Instead I duck back around the corner and go to class the other way. Then I wish I had talked to him.

I'm thinking about trying to catch up with him after school. (I know. This is not the relationship tactic *Cosmo* would recommend.) Unfortunately, or fortunately, Mr. Arthur catches me on the way out of his classroom. He wants me to join his Wednesday afternoon study group for extra math help. "Christmas exams will sneak up on you," he says.

It's only November. And thinking to the end of the week stresses me out at the moment — I can't handle thinking about the end of term.

I tell Mr. Arthur I'll consider it. By the time I escape him, the hallways are clearing and Jerome's gone.

Waiting outside for me is my dad. He's sitting in his hideously embarrassing green Volvo station wagon (which he says has cachet, whatever that's supposed to mean) and he's scanning the lawn for me. He's dressed for work, in creased black pants and a golf shirt. At the office he adds a lab coat and stethoscope.

"Dad, what are you doing here?"

"I had a couple of cancellations. Came to pick you up," he says, like it's the most normal thing in the world.

"Last time you picked me up from school I was eight and it was so cold outside that kids were getting frostbite waiting for the bus."

He just grunts. "Want to come for a drive or not?"

This is what happens when you're the only child of a single parent. Any other father who found himself with an afternoon off would probably call his wife. But not my dad. He hardly ever has a girlfriend even. And he's a pretty good catch — a doctor, wonderful daughter (of course), a big house. The shag carpet's a downside, but I'm sure a girlfriend could change that.

We get out of town pretty fast. There are only four traffic lights in all of Fairfield, so it's not like there's a big afternoon traffic jam. Soon we're winding up Bow Creek Road. There's no snow on the ground, but the trees are bare and the branches look crisp, like they've stiffened in the cold.

"Dad, where are you taking me?"

"Patience. You'll see soon."

He used to do this when I was a little kid. He'd pick up take-out fried chicken and pop and drive up one of the old logging roads around town until he found a picnic spot. But we haven't done that in years, and it's going to be dark in a couple of hours.

He pulls off the road near a driveway with a gate across it. "Come on," he says.

"Dad — no trespassing!"

"Since when are you such a goody two-shoes? Where's your investigative drive?" he teases, jumping the gate.

"No one has said goody two-shoes since *Leave it to Beaver* went off the air in the seventies," I grumble as I follow him. The driveway ends at a gravel turnaround, but Dad continues down a rough trail. I can hear a river through the trees. "Almost there," he says.

I crunch along behind him, complaining about wood ticks. Two minutes later we emerge from the trees — at the top of a cliff. My dad has his arm out to slow me down.

"Go to the edge on your stomach," he says.

We both drop and wiggle forward to where we can see into the canyon. There's a huge waterfall below. To the right, where the walls of the canyon gradually narrow, the water is calm and glassy. Then it roars over the cliff, and it never recovers. It's all whirlpools and rapids at the base.

"This was your mom's favorite spot before she moved back to the city," Dad tells me, sliding back from the edge.

"It's incredible."

"She said it was a good place to escape her problems."

I can understand that. Even when I move back from the edge and lie in the tiny clearing, I can still see the spray of water rising. When I close my eyes, the roar makes me dizzy, as if the cliff might give way any minute.

I can understand why my mom had things to escape. This town, for example, where everyone knows everything about you. She grew up in the city. I guess the life of a small-town doctor's wife was more claustrophobic than she expected.

She's never said that. When I see her — usually in the summer or at Christmas — she just avoids talking about Fairfield.

"I saw Officer McBride yesterday," Dad says.

"Really?" That's enough to make me open my eyes and sit up.

"Just for coffee. But he mentioned the Granville murder."

"Really?" That's all I seem to be able to say.

"They don't seem to be making much headway. Trouble finding information, he says."

"I'd heard that." I am noncommittal. I am completely calm. Deep breath. Maybe taking up yoga would be a good idea.

"The interesting thing is this," Dad continues. "He seems to think that a lot of people know exactly what went on that night. He thinks there's a good chance the entire high school knows who murdered Ted Granville."

"That's an exaggeration," I say.

Dad looks up from a fallen leaf he's been shredding. "Do you know?" he asks.

"I never saw it." I shrug. "I was downstairs."

"I believe you didn't see it happen," Dad says. "But this is a small town. It's hard to keep secrets, especially when you're seventeen."

"If someone saw it, they would never tell the cops. They'd probably end up like Ted Granville by the next day."

"I'm sure the police would protect anyone with information," Dad says confidently.

"Whatever. What about that woman on the news last year who had a restraining order against her husband? He broke into her house and killed her."

Dad looks at me like I'm being unreasonable. "If you know something, you need to tell me."

These are the thoughts that go through my head, in fast-forward:

Ross's boots.

Ross leaning over me in the hallway.

Jerome's silence.

Jerome's "I had a really shitty day."

Jerome's "What if your dad killed someone? What if he asked you to lie?"

"No," I tell my dad, making myself look right in his eyes, "I don't know who it was. I'm sure someone at school knows, but most people would rather not."

Chapter Six

Georgia seems to have forgiven me for not explaining my breakup. She was a bit distant at lunch yesterday, but today she's back to normal. I guess she's decided that I'll tell her eventually.

We're talking in the hallway when Scott finds us. He nods at Georgia, then leans in close to me. "I have a new story angle. Can you meet me at lunch? Maybe 12:30 in the media lab?"

I nod, and the bell rings for homeroom.

As the grade nine student-of-the-week reads the announcements over the P.A., Mr. Arthur hands a note to Georgia and one to me. It seems we both have appointments with the school counselor tomorrow. I roll my eyes while Georgia pretends she's going to puke.

I'm in the lab at 12:30 on the dot, waiting for Scott. I'm still there at 12:40, 12:50 and 1:00, when the bell rings. I don't see him in the halls all afternoon, but that's not unusual. I assume he forgot about our meeting. I do see Ian between classes, sporting a puffy black eye, but I don't have time to ask him about it.

My dad is waiting in the parking lot after school again.

"Is this a new trend?" I joke.

"Scott Rich is in the hospital."

"What?" I throw my bag in the backseat and jump in. "What are you talking about? I saw him this morning!"

"Well he obviously met with trouble

since then. He was assaulted. I was doing rounds at the hospital and happened to hear. Thought you might want to go up."

Dad parks near the entrance. As soon as we push through the double doors, that hospital smell of disinfectant and pee and paint hits me. I hate hospitals. The only time I ever stayed in one was to have my tonsils out in grade nine. I haven't been able to eat Jell-O since. The girl in the bed next to me kept throwing up. They closed the curtains around her, but I could still hear her. Ugh.

Dad checks with the nurse before we go in. She says Scott will be fine. He's got a broken wrist and a concussion, but nothing that won't heal.

"Don't stay long," she warns. "He needs his rest."

Dad walks me to the door of Scott's room, then wanders off to wait in the lounge.

As soon as I step in, I want to turn around and leave. Both of Scott's eyes are black. One eyebrow's sliced open and his bottom lip is swollen. His arm's in a cast.

"Hey," he says. It comes out like the voice of a bad ventriloquist, through lips that barely move.

"I just heard, and I came right up. How bad does it hurt?"

"I'm pretty doped up."

I perch on the edge of the bed so he doesn't have to talk loudly. "If you wanted bigger lips, you could have tried a collagen injection."

He starts to smile, but he winces.

"What happened?"

"It's nothing. Disgruntled ex-boyfriend of a girl I'm seeing."

"A girl you're seeing? I thought you were madly in love with me." I'm only teasing, but Scott *is* pretty hot in an intellectual sort of way.

Scott doesn't smile at my joke, so I change tactics. "Is that what you told the cops? That an angry ex beat you up?"

He nods. I can tell even that hurts.

"Liar. You said you were working a new story angle."

He doesn't say anything.

"Did Ross do this? Jerome? Nate?"

"Jen, don't get involved."

"This isn't just your story. I'm already involved."

He closes his eyes for a minute. "It's my own fault. I wasn't careful."

"It was not your fault."

"You know, after he hit me, when I thought I was going to pass out, he leaned down and whispered, 'Silence is the best policy.' It was creepy."

"Who whispered, Scott?"

"Guess," he says.

We sit quietly for a few minutes, but he grabs my hand when I move off the bed to go. "Jen?"

"Yeah?" I can tell he's trying to decide something. Scott's the kind of old-fashioned guy who will put his arm in front of you at crosswalks until he's sure it's safe to cross. Finally, he decides to risk it.

"There's something I left in the lab," he says.

My dad raises his bushy eyebrows at me when I find him in the lounge.

"Jealous ex-boyfriend of a girl he's seeing," I tell him.

"He can press charges for that," Dad says.

"He knows."

Chapter Seven

These are the things in my locker when I arrive at school on Thursday morning: seven binders; one apple, slightly bruised; emergency bag containing a brush, gum, two tampons, and a bottle of aspirin; one embarrassing picture of a male model's body with Jerome's head pasted on top (Georgia taped it up and I've never torn it down); a few copies of the latest *Fair Game* shows. Lying on top of the videos is a folded piece of red paper. Someone must have stuffed it through the vents at the top of the locker.

In thick black pen it says, "Silence is the best policy."

I drop it. Then I snatch it up again like it might contaminate my locker.

Okay. Think like a journalist, I tell myself. I take off my backpack and rummage around for the cookies I put in this morning. Dumping them out of their plastic bag, I shake out the crumbs and put the note inside.

With the note safely stowed, I stand up. Georgia has appeared at the locker beside me and she's holding a red note in front of her with two fingers, as if it's anthrax-infected.

"Put that away," I hiss.

"What does it mean?"

"Come here." I pull her into homeroom, which is still deserted. I shut the door and we perch on top of the desks, facing each other.

"Georgia, you can't breathe a word of this

to anyone. Not even Nate. Not anyone. Understand?"

She nods solemnly.

"You won't mention it to anyone at lunch? Even if other people have notes?"

"I couldn't even if I wanted to. Counselor's appointment. Mine's noon and yours is 12:30, remember?"

Damn. I hadn't remembered.

Quickly, I fill her in on everything that's happened — Scott's beating, Ross's little talk with me in the hallway, my breakup with Jerome. It feels good to spill my guts to someone. Georgia doesn't seem that surprised by my information.

"I have a secret to tell you, too," she says.

"Really?"

"Remember that guy, Rocky, who was beaten up last year?"

I nod. Rocky is a couple of years older than us, but he still hangs out at a lot of the teenage parties. Last year he got beaten up so badly he was in the hospital for a week. Everyone wanted him to press charges, but he would never tell anyone who attacked him. He said it was a misunderstanding — no big deal.

"That was Ross," Georgia says.

"How do you know?"

"Nate told me. He says Ross can't handle the steroids he's taking. He's got a bad temper to begin with, and now when someone pisses him off, things get out of control."

"Disgusting. Why would anyone take those things?"

Georgia shrugs. "To get bigger, I guess."

"Is Nate on them?"

She shrugs again.

I suddenly remember one more thing I haven't told Georgia — Officer McBride's information about the boot prints. Her eyebrows go up when she hears.

"You think that might be a print from Ross's boots?"

I nod.

"And you think either Nate or Jerome is involved?"

I have time for another quick nod, but

that's the end of our conversation — the bell rings, the classroom door bangs open and everyone begins filing into homeroom.

I have a long, dull morning of geography and math. English gets a little more interesting. Someone does a class presentation on the *Macbeth* witches, all about how their predictions were full of tricks and double meanings.

And even more interesting, I find out from Georgia afterwards that everyone who was at Ian's party has a counselor's appointment.

"Why now?" I whisper. "Why not last week?"

She rolls her eyes. "Maybe because Mrs. Bing didn't want to deal with real problems?"

Mrs. Bing has been the high school counselor since the age of dinosaurs. The only time I ever see her is at assemblies. She usually drones on about some school problem she's suddenly become aware of — drinking, for example. Last year there was an uproar when a grade nine girl fainted in class. Mrs. Bing, convinced this was a case of anorexia, started stuffing soda crackers in her mouth. The poor girl was lucky she didn't choke. She turned out to be hypoglycemic.

When I get to my 12:30 appointment, I'm already unhappy at having to skip the second half of today's *Fair Game* meeting.

The counselor's office has no desk. There are four of the big principal's office-style chairs around a low table. It looks ideal for a parent-teacher meeting.

Mrs. Bing is cutting out letters for some sort of bulletin board display. She's got grey hair set in curls tight to her head, and her bifocals are pushed down on her nose. She motions me to sit.

"I suppose you're wondering why I asked you to meet me, Jen."

"I figured it was the murder."

She puts down her scissors and looks at me as if deciding whether I'm going to be difficult or not.

I don't give her time to decide. "If you're so concerned, why didn't you call us in here right after it happened? It's been two weeks."

Mrs. Bing leans forward. "I'll be honest with you, Jen."

That irritates me more. I hate it when people use my name in every sentence, like that's going to make us best friends.

"The thing is, Jen," she's saying, "the police have asked the school to become more actively involved in this situation. First, they believe there were student witnesses to the murder, and they would like to speak with them. Second, they suspect there might be some bullying going on, and none of us want that, Jen."

"No, Mrs. Bing. None of us want that." I think of the note someone left in my locker and for a split second I consider showing it to her. Then I remember what a spaz Mrs. Bing is. Within minutes she'll have word of "bullying" all over the school. She'll be yapping about how well she's dealing with it, and somehow everyone will know that *I* turned in the note.

"Then let's continue . . ." Mrs. Bing

moves on to questions about the party, the other kids at the party, where I went afterwards. It's really just a slow-motion repeat of the police interview, with more emphasis on the touchy-feely, how-are-you-coping aspects.

At the end, I haven't told her anything new. When I leave, she seems a bit defeated. I could tell her right now that the rest of these meetings will be a waste of time.

With all of this delving (on Mrs. Bing's part) and ducking (on mine), I don't have time alone in the lab at lunch. It's not until the end of the day that I make my way there. Someone's been editing film, and the lights are off. The room glows faintly from the thin slices of light that flow through the closed blinds.

On the far side, past the counter with its editing equipment and computer monitors, there's a four-drawer filing cabinet. The top drawer has Scott's name on it. The tape I'm looking for is right on top, resting on last week's notes.

I look around the room. Everyone on the news staff had an introduction to the equipment at the beginning of the year, but I haven't edited anything since — I concentrate on the interviews and let other people do the technical work. Luckily, I find a VCR that plays normally to one of the monitors. Hoping I'm not accidentally erasing anything, I press play — and get last week's basketball game. Stop. Rewind. Try again.

"Let this be it. Let this be it," I whisper to myself as I press play again. It is.

At first the shot's a bit out of focus, but the camera adjusts. It's a great scene, with just the right amount of shadow around the three figures and just the right amount of white in the cinder blocks behind them. Part of the corner of the building is visible, as if Scott is hiding out of sight. Now he zooms closer, and I notice more details. The violence in Ross's eyes as he holds Ian against the wall outside the school. The threat from Nate as he leans towards them. He must be saying something. Ian has a piece of duct tape across his mouth. No black eye, yet. He looks terrified. It's obvious no one has spotted Scott.

"What happened? Did they see you? Was Jerome there?" I've gone straight from the media lab to the hospital. I have so many questions that I barely give Scott time to talk. I notice that he's looking better, though. The swelling around his eyes has gone down.

"They have no idea I got those shots. I ran back inside and stashed the tape in the lab, then I went to help Ian. By the time I got there he had a black eye, maybe some broken ribs. He's okay, though."

"You should have called for help," I tell him.

He nods. "I thought I'd pretend to happen upon them and that Ross would back off." Another shrug. "He didn't. I think he assumed I knew what they were talking about. I should never have gotten involved."

"Maybe Ian was threatening to turn them in," I say.

"Do you think I should have told the cops?" Scott asks.

"I don't know. What if they didn't believe you? What if Ross found out what you'd told them? You'd probably be dead right now."

"I keep thinking about that investigator, too," he says. "The big one at Ian's house the first time we were filming there? He looked like he was ready to believe we were guilty just because we're the right age."

"Don't remind me." I tell Scott about Officer Behnson's threat as I left the interrogation room.

I don't have any suggestions for Scott, so there's not much to talk about. I sit by his bed for a few minutes and bring him some magazines from the lounge.

When I get home, it's almost seven. My dad's been waiting, worried.

Chapter Eight

Lady Macbeth sucks. It's late on Sunday night and I've done absolutely nothing all weekend. Now I have my English books in bed with me.

It's lucky that my presentation isn't until Friday, because I'm not getting anywhere. I'm supposed to do a ten-minute spiel about Lady Macbeth's strengths. I keep reading her part in the play, and I think she had more weaknesses. First she plots a murder. I admit, that took guts. But then she feels so guilty that she sleepwalks all over the castle, rubbing imaginary blood off her hands. She dies before the final battle begins. What kind of strength is that? She helped create the mess in the first place. She should have done something.

I should do something.

I chuck my English books off my bed and grab a blank piece of paper. I write:

Reasons to go to the police

• If I don't, someone's going to get away with murder.

• Some people deserve to know the truth — Ted Granville's wife, for example.

• I have evidence: Ross's missing boots, Scott's videotape.

• Ross shouldn't be going around intimidating people, beating them up and leaving notes in their lockers.

I cross out the first two reasons for being too much like things Pollyanna would say.

It's the last two things on the list that make me want to tell.

Reasons never to go to the police

- I'll eventually have to tell Dad I lied to him about not knowing anything.
- Someone might see me at the station. Word might get out that I've gone to the cops.
- It might get Jerome in more trouble.
- I'll have to see the cops all smirking, congratulating themselves on thinking I was involved.

My conclusions: I am paranoid-delusional (do I really think they've got someone watching the door of the police station? This is not a horror movie). It seems I also have love-sick-puppy syndrome for Jerome. I cross out the entire list and write, "You are a freak. You are a freak. You are a freak," in multicolored pens down the rest of the page.

All of this leaves me where I started. I should do something. What? I turn off the light and lie on my back, thinking. Then I lie on my stomach, thinking. Then on my side. It takes me a long time to fall asleep.

Let's hear it for osmosis, the art of gaining wisdom while unconscious. I hadn't decided anything when I finally fell asleep last night, but this morning I know exactly what I'm going to do. All that's left is to convince Scott. Of course, getting him out of the hospital would help, too. I make my plans as I walk to school. By the time I get there, I'm smiling in smug satisfaction.

Then I see Jerome waiting for me in the hallway, and my smile slides off my face like oil-based makeup.

Deep breath.

"Hey," he says. I wait for more, but that seems to be all he's going to say. He just stands against my locker, looking at me.

"Could I help you with something?"

"No. Well, yes," he says, with a goofy grin. "I've missed you."

Did I mention how good-looking Jerome is?

That's almost the end of all my plans for justice. My ideas from the walk to school this morning go skittering off down the hallway like a bunch of half-hatched eggs. How could

I have considered doing anything that might get Jerome in trouble? Besides, it's obvious he would never do anything wrong.

I'm just opening my mouth to tell Jerome that I miss him too, when I see Ian's battered face coming down the hall. When I look back at Jerome, I'm wondering whether this is a strategy to keep me quiet. I might be getting back together with a could-be-murderer.

My "I miss you" turns into "I gotta go."

I duck past him and head to the only reasonable place — the girls' washroom. I brush by Georgia, and she follows me in.

"This is terrible!"

"It's just a bad day," she soothes.

"It's not just a bad day! I just refused to go out with Jerome, and I visited my favorite non-boyfriend boyfriend in the hospital."

"Boys suck" is all Georgia can think of to say.

I'm all snotty and blotchy when the bell rings. We both miss first period, and Georgia makes me promise to have lunch with her at Willie's Chicken.

All that grease combined with a chocolate milkshake revives me a bit, and by the afternoon I manage to walk serenely by Jerome in the hallway.

With all the hysterics, I don't have time for my plan. I don't even think about it again until last period — English. It's someone else's presentation today, and it's about the role of prophecy in the play. The plans of Macbeth and Lady M. are unraveling, and the signs are pointing to defeat. You have to like Shakespearean endings — all blood and last-minute honor. I tune out and concentrate on how I'm going to convince Scott to help.

As soon as class is over, I make a quick stop in the media lab. Then I head for the hospital.

"Scott," I say, starting to talk before I'm even through the door to his room, "I know you're not going to like this, but…"

"It's about time you got here," he interrupts. "I need to talk to you because we've got to do something."

"What?"

"I knew you wouldn't want to, so I've been thinking all afternoon of how to convince you."

"How to convince me to do what?"

"An exposé," he says.

"But that's my idea!"

"What?"

Obviously we're having some communication problems. When we slow down long enough to listen to each other, it turns out that we've both made almost identical plans.

"But I thought you wanted to leave things alone," I tell him.

"I did. But the longer I lie here with nothing to do except think, the more angry I get. Who died and made Ross king? Who gives him the right to do something like this? It's either the exposé or I go after him myself."

"Wow. I mean, I always thought of you as a passive sort of guy," I say.

"Yeah," he nods, grinning. "It's probably better that we choose the exposé option."

Ten minutes later I have the camera set

up on a tripod, and I'm holding the microphone beside his hospital bed.

"Mr. Rich," I begin, in my most professional reporter voice, "you say you were beaten by two students of Fairfield Secondary?"

"Ross Reed and Nate Schultz."

"And the reason for this attack?"

"I saw them intimidating another student — Ian Klassen."

"In your mind, do these attacks relate to the recent murder of local banker Ted Granville?"

We go on like this for another ten minutes. We probably could have filmed for longer, but someone else turned up at the door — Georgia.

"What are you doing here? Are you okay?" For once, Georgia doesn't look like she's walked out of a fashion magazine. Her face is white and her eyes are red. She looks like she might throw up. Instead, she tosses a plastic bag she's carrying onto the end of Scott's bed.

"What's this?" he asks.

"The boots."

I'm shocked into silence. Scott merely looks confused, and I remember that I never told him Officer McBride's secret about the boot print.

"How did you get these?" I ask her.

"I was over at Nate's last week and we were, well, fooling around in the basement. When I went to go to the washroom, I accidentally walked into the storage room. These were in a pile of junk. I only noticed them because I knew they were Ross's. I thought he must have forgotten them there."

"So how did you get them?"

"After you told me what the cops said…"

"What did the cops say?" Scott wonders. We ignore him.

"I skipped class this afternoon and went to his house," Georgia continues. "He's got a key stashed in the carport for when he sneaks in at night. I just ducked in and grabbed them."

"That took guts," Scott says approvingly. "But what's so important about the boots?"

We fill him in, finally. Then I give Georgia a hug and make her promise to be careful.

That's all the time I have to worry about her. Scott's out of the hospital tomorrow, and he'll edit our exposé tape. My job, meanwhile, is to film the boots and write some narrative to run over top, explaining their significance. I'm also supposed to interview a police representative about the progress of the investigation.

By lunchtime on Thursday, we're finished. Scott has done even better than he planned — he's called Ian and managed to get the call on tape. Ian practically admits to seeing Granville beaten.

Now all we need to do is get it on the air. Ms. Chan will never let us run it without watching it first. We decide we'll have to secretly replace the *Fair Game* tape that's supposed to air tomorrow — Teen Smoking — with our exposé. Ms. Chan takes the tapes to the cable station every Thursday evening, so we have to make the switch right after school.

"You ready?" Scott asks, when he meets me by my locker.

"Ready." I tuck the tape inside one of my binders and clutch it to my chest. We walk side by side to the lab, not saying anything. I'm not even breathing, though I don't notice until we walk into the lab and find it deserted. Then I feel like my body starts working again. Adrenaline is flowing through me.

"Where's the Teen Smoking tape?" I ask.

"She usually keeps them up here, on top of the filing cabinet." Scott moves some papers, and there's the cassette.

"Okay, give it to me. Here's the exposé."

"The what?" Ms. Chan has walks into the lab behind us. Scott jumps. I'm so nervous I scream, and that's the end of any chance we have at a cover-up.

Ms. Chan looks more stern than I've ever seen her. "Would you like to explain what's going on here?"

She looks first at me, then at Scott.

"Well…" I stutter. "There's this…"

Scott shrugs. "You may as well just watch the tape."

Chapter Nine

We pull the blinds, and Scott pops the cassette into the machine. Ms. Chan still looks pissed, but she sits down to watch.

Scott's done an amazing job of the editing. The show starts with me interviewing him at the hospital. Then, while our voices continue over top, the video switches to the scene of Ian being beaten outside the school. After that, the police interview and a shot of

Ross's boots. Finally, the phone call to Ian, over a lonely, creepy shot of the murder scene.

"Were you an eyewitness to this murder?" the me-on-tape asks the Scott-on-tape as the show closes.

"No," he says. "Were you?"

Then he looks straight into the camera. "Were you?"

Fade to black.

Ms. Chan watches the entire thing in silence. We stare at her in the semi-dark, waiting for her reaction.

"The principal should see this," she says finally.

"No!" both Scott and I shout at the same time.

"Ms. Chan," Scott continues more calmly, "unless everyone sees this at the same time, unless *everyone* sees it, Jen and I are in deep shit."

"What if it never airs?" I add, panicking. "What if the principal takes it to the police, and Ross finds out?"

She's quiet again, then she nods. "Let me make a phone call," she says. When we both look doubtful, she adds, "I promise not to put either of you in danger. Stay here. I shouldn't be too long."

Once Ms. Chan has gone, I open the blinds to let in the light from the classroom. Scott and I slump in the chairs.

I'm the first to speak. "Scott?"

"Yeah?"

"We know Ross beat up Ted Granville, right?"

"Yeah."

"And we know there were two people involved."

"Yeah."

"Do you think the second person was Nate or . . . Jerome?"

Once I've asked the question, I don't think I want to know the answer.

Scott doesn't answer anyway. He nods towards the classroom outside and says, "I guess you can ask him yourself."

Jerome.

"I've been looking all over for you," Jerome says as he comes through the door. "And I'm not the only one. Come on, we've gotta go."

"I'm not going anywhere with you," I tell him.

"Look, they know you're up to something. And they have a pretty good idea what it is."

Both Scott and I sit up. "Who? And what do they know?"

"Ross and Nate. Ian saw you filming outside his house, and he told them. And he told them about your phone call," he says, looking at Scott.

"Why would he tell them that?" Scott asks.

"Scared, I guess. But look, we've got to go. It really isn't safe for the three of us to be alone like this."

"Too late," I tell him. Ross has just walked in.

"Jerome," he says, "get out of the way."

"Don't be an asshole about this," Jerome says.

"Back off."

Jerome stays where he is. "Come on, Ross. Let's just get out of here. Someone's going to find us."

"Good idea," Ross says, looking only at Scott and me. "Let's get out of here together, and then I'll decide what to do about you two."

"I'm not going anywhere," I say again.

"And it's three of you against one of me," Ross says. Very calmly, he takes a knife out of his jacket pocket. "I say we all leave together."

"Holy shit," Scott mutters.

"You could get expelled!" I gasp. Then I realize how stupid that is. Getting expelled is the least of Ross's worries.

Suddenly I see Ms. Chan in the doorway. Her mouth drops. Then she's gone. Did I imagine her? I look quickly at Ross and Jerome. They haven't noticed anything.

"Get up," Ross says, motioning to Scott

and me. "Pick up that stuff and bring it with you." We do exactly as he says. I grab the cassette, and Scott hoists the video camera.

"Let's calm down here," Jerome says, stalling.

"This is not the time to switch sides," Ross replies. Suddenly the knife is pointing at Jerome. It's a hunting knife, and so close to my face that I can see the light glinting on the edge.

Everything seems to slow, and there's time for a thousand miscellaneous thoughts to run through my head. I've never seen anyone pull a knife before. On TV, maybe. This is not the same. Definitely not the same. At least it's not a gun. This is exactly the type of thing that makes people wet their pants. That would be embarrassing. If I live long enough to be embarrassed. Where will Ross take us if we leave here?

For a second I think I must be imagining it, but then Ross turns his head slightly to listen. There's a siren in the distance. Have we been here for seconds or minutes? Did

"I'm sorry I got you involved in all this," he said, almost before saying hello.

"You didn't get me involved. We were all part of it as soon as we showed up at the party that night."

"Maybe."

"I'm glad you didn't get shot."

"You thought I got shot?"

"I didn't know what happened until we were all at the police station. I had to explain *everything* to Officer Wells before he would tell me what happened in the classroom."

"Ross raised the knife. I don't know what he was thinking. He got shot in the shoulder."

"Good aim. I guess you're not under arrest for murder, either," I said, with a question in my voice.

"I still might be charged with conspiracy or something. But I'm fine with that. I'm just glad it's over. And Jen…" he paused.

"I don't want us to be fighting," he said finally.

I didn't answer. Instead I asked, "Did you see them beat up Ted Granville?"

"Most of it."

"Can you explain how it happened? Why no one stopped them?"

"At the beginning it seemed like no big deal. He wasn't the type of guy Ross would usually go around beating up, but he really pissed Ross off. Ian's parents must have asked Granville to keep an eye on the house while they were away. He came upstairs like he owned the place and found Ian, Ross, Nate and me hanging out. He told everyone to get out.

"Ross had been drinking. No more than anyone else, but you know how he gets when the drinks and the steroids kick in and someone gets in his way. He said there was no way he was leaving. Who was going to make him? It just escalated from there. Ross pushed the guy, the guy pushed back, then Ross slugged him. Nate got in on it. Ian took off, like he wanted to pretend he'd never been there in the first place."

"And what did you do?" I asked.

"Well, at first I was cheering them on. I wasn't getting into it myself, but that guy had been a jerk. I figured he was getting what he deserved. Then things got out of control. He was down on the ground, not fighting back anymore. Ross and Nate kept kicking him. I yelled at them to cool it, but they didn't listen. Finally I pulled Ross off, and then Nate stopped. He looked like he hadn't realized what he was doing to the guy."

"Where did they go after? I didn't see Ross leave."

"The first thing Ross said was that he had to get out of there. He knew he'd be the first suspect. He climbed out the window and took off. Nate and I decided we should leave and mingle in the rest of the party like nothing had happened."

"What about calling the police? The ambulance? What if he'd still been alive?"

Jerome sighed. "I guess we just weren't thinking straight. Our only plan was to look shocked when someone found him. It didn't take more than a few minutes anyway — Candi saw the body as soon as she came upstairs."

We were quiet for a minute, listening

only to the faint buzz of the phone line. Finally, Jerome whispered, "So we're okay? We're back to normal?"

I almost laughed. Did he really think things were going back to normal? "I don't think so, Jerome. But I'm glad you're okay."

"It wasn't me, Jen. And I need you right now."

"Good luck with things, okay?" It was a lame thing to say, I know. But I couldn't talk to him anymore. I hung up before he could say anything else. The phone rang again right after, but I yelled at Dad not to answer.

Dad's staying home from work, which is a first. I don't ever remember him canceling appointments before. He's sitting at the dining room table reading medical research articles with a highlighter in his hand. Every once in a while he glances over at me, like he wants to make sure I'm still there.

"Stop looking at me like that!" I say finally. "You're giving me the creeps."

He sighs. "I'm glad you're okay."

"I'm fine."

"You should have talked to me about this, you know. You could have told me. What you did was dangerous."

"What if you hadn't believed me?"

He gets up and walks over to the couch. "I would have. I promise you — I would have believed you."

"Okay, okay," I shrug, grinning up at him. "Next time."

"There better not *be* a next time."

Any more mushy father-daughter talk is interrupted by the doorbell. Without waiting for us to answer, Scott and Georgia come in, undoing jackets and scarves as they go.

"It's freezing out there!" Georgia says, extra-loudly as if to make everything seem normal. "It's supposed to snow tonight."

Scott doesn't say anything at first. He looks tentative, like he's not sure whether to touch me or not.

My dad must see us looking at each other. In a sudden fit of diplomacy, he excuses himself.

"Why don't I pour some drinks?" he says. "Georgia, could you give me a hand?"

"Was Nate arrested?" I ask as soon as they're gone.

Scott nods. "They took Ross to the hospital yesterday, but there's a cop outside his door. They arrested Nate at his house."

"Did you give Ross's boots to the police?"

He nods again. "I haven't heard if they were useful. The police aren't releasing any information. On the news they said they had two suspects in custody. They can't even release their names."

I can hear Georgia and my dad talking in the kitchen. They seem to have gotten deep into conversation and forgotten about us. They're probably talking about me.

Scott sits on the arm of the couch and reaches for my hand. He plays with it for a minute, not looking at me. "Now that Jerome's not a murderer, are you back together?" he asks.

"*Technically* he's not a murderer," I say

bitterly. "But he didn't exactly rush to call an ambulance, did he? He watched someone die. He stood there and let him bleed to death."

Scott doesn't answer. I follow his eyes. Dad and Georgia are standing in the doorway, their faces matching pictures of shock and disgust. It's like we're all trying not to think about what happened. Then we remember, and we picture the floor, the body, the blood.

Scott drops my hand.

My head begins to feel heavy again and my dad clears his throat. "We all need some time," he says in his best professional doctor voice. "Why don't you two stop by again some other time?"

"I'll call you?" Scott asks me at the doorway.

"That would be good. But give me a while, okay?" I say softly.

Georgia leans over to give me a hug.

"You did a good thing," she says.

"You *did* do a good thing," my dad nods

after the door has closed behind them. "Of course, you're grounded for the rest of your life." At least he smiles as he says it.